Jul 2016

STORIES OF THE CIVIL RIGHTS MOVEMENT

JAMES MEREDITH
AND THE UNIVERSITY OF MISSISSIPPI

by Karen Latchana Kenney

Content Consultant
Keith Mayes, PhD
African American and African Studies
University of Minnesota

Core Library
An Imprint of Abdo Publishing
abdopublishing.com

abdopublishing.com

Published by Abdo Publishing, a division of ABDO, PO Box 398166, Minneapolis, Minnesota 55439. Copyright © 2016 by Abdo Consulting Group, Inc. International copyrights reserved in all countries. No part of this book may be reproduced in any form without written permission from the publisher. Core Library™ is a trademark and logo of Abdo Publishing.

Printed in the United States of America, North Mankato, Minnesota

042015
092015

Cover Photo: AP Images
Interior Photos: AP Images, 1, 7, 20, 22, 26, 34; Bettmann/Corbis, 4, 12, 28, 30, 43, 45; Horace Cort/AP Images, 14; Marion Post Walcott/Picture History/Newscom, 17; Jim Bourdier/AP Images, 18; Fred Waters/AP Images, 36; Everett Collection/Newscom, 38

Editor: Jon Westmark
Series Designer: Becky Daum

Library of Congress Control Number: 2015931192

Cataloging-in-Publication Data
Kenney, Karen Latchana.
 James Meredith and the University of Mississippi / Karen Latchana Kenney.
   p. cm. -- (Stories of the civil rights movement)
Includes bibliographical references and index.
ISBN 978-1-62403-879-2
1. University of Mississippi--History--Juvenile literature. 2. College integration--Mississippi--Oxford--History--Juvenile literature. 3. African Americans--Civil rights--Mississippi--Oxford--History--Juvenile literature.
I. Title.
378.762/83--dc23
                                          2015931192

CONTENTS

CHAPTER ONE

CONFLICT ON CAMPUS

S unday, September 30, 1962, was quiet in the small town of Oxford, Mississippi. On the campus of the University of Mississippi, nearly half the students were gone for the weekend. But the stillness was broken at approximately 3:30 p.m. Planes roared toward the town's airport. They carried 536 law enforcement officers. Something big was about to happen at the university known as Ole Miss.

Federal marshals exit an airplane in Oxford, Mississippi, on September 30, 1962.

The officers were coming to protect an African-American man named James Meredith. The young man wanted to register for classes at the previously all-white college. He had applied and had been accepted to Ole Miss after a long court battle.

The US government had ordered the school to allow Meredith to attend. But Mississippi Governor Ross Barnett was disobeying those orders. He vowed to keep Meredith from signing up for classes. Many whites throughout Mississippi were also against Meredith's enrollment.

The officers arrived at the school a little after 4:00 p.m. They

Barnett's Mixed Messages

Governor Barnett told President John F. Kennedy that he would obey federal orders. But he sent a different message to the people of Mississippi. He told them he supported segregation. And when the riot at Ole Miss was starting, he made a radio address. He told the public that federal officers had brought Meredith onto school grounds. He asked the crowd to avoid violence. But he also said that the US government was oppressive.

Government officers form a line around the Lyceum as a crowd gathers.

surrounded the main building on campus, called the Lyceum. Approximately 400 people stood outside. Most were students. They wanted to protest Meredith's admittance to the school. The crowd grew to several thousand as the night went on. Many nonstudents joined. The head of the university urged the people to go back to their homes. But the crowd did not listen.

What the crowd did not know was that Meredith was already there. He had been secretly brought on

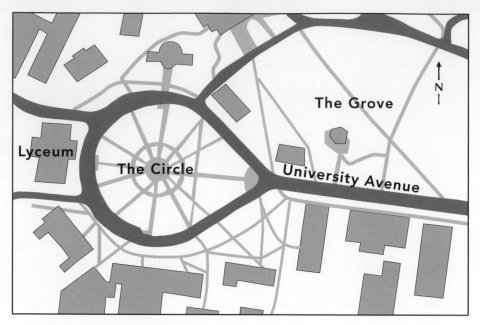

Ole Miss Campus

This map shows the campus of Ole Miss. After reading about the start of the riot at Ole Miss, what does this map help you understand about the event? Based on the map, where might protesters have gathered near the Lyceum?

campus. He was waiting in Baxter Hall, away from the Lyceum building and crowd. Meredith was waiting there until he could register on Monday morning. He had tried before to register, but Barnett had blocked his attempts. But this time Meredith had federal support on campus. He believed this time it would work.

The Mississippi Highway Patrol was also on school grounds. They were supposed to help keep the peace. At approximately 7:30 p.m., the crowd began throwing rocks, pipes, bottles, and bricks at the federal officers. The highway patrol left when this happened. The patrol was under Barnett's control. The remaining federal officers were outnumbered and unprepared to fight the angry mob.

Just before 8:00 p.m., the officers fired tear gas

CIVIL RIGHTS VOICES
James Meredith

I had known that I belonged to a group that was distinctly different from at least one other group, but until I was fifteen I did not know that my group was supposed to be the inferior one.

James Meredith was born in 1933 in Attala County, Mississippi. Between 1961 and 1962, he applied a number of times to attend Ole Miss. But he was denied because of his race. After being allowed to attend, Meredith graduated from Ole Miss in 1963. He later earned a master's degree and a law degree at other schools. Meredith has written books and worked in politics. He continues to work for civil rights.

to try to break up the crowd. This was the start of a riot that would turn the school into a battlefield. Soon the US National Guard was brought in. The riot lasted until 2:00 a.m. By then two people were dead and more than 300 were hurt.

Yet on Monday morning, October 1, Chief US Marshal James McShane and Justice Department attorney John Doar walked with Meredith to the Lyceum building. He registered for five classes. At 9:00 a.m., Meredith sat in his first class at Ole Miss.

Fighting for Change

The events at Ole Miss were part of a larger movement in the United States. The civil rights movement fought to gain equal rights for African Americans. During the 1950s and 1960s, protests and legal battles brought national attention to the differences in how whites and African Americans were treated. Meredith's fight to attend Ole Miss was one victory in this movement. It led to the integration of Ole Miss.

A *New York Times* article described the destruction caused by rioters on the night of September 30, 1962:

> *Bricks, lumber and other building materials were stolen from a construction site and used as missiles or roadblocks. The rioters ripped up the garden of a home. . . . Virtually all the street lights were shot out or broken by rocks early in the evening. Observers . . . got a view of shadowy forms racing back and forth behind Confederate battle flags. The rioters cranked up the bulldozer twice and sent it crashing driverless toward the marshals. Both times it hit trees and other obstructions that stopped it before it reached their ranks.*
>
> Source: Claude Sitton. "Shots Quell Mob; Enrolling of Meredith Ends Segregation in State Schools." New York Times October 2, 1962. Print. 1.

What's the Big Idea?

Read this passage closely. What does it describe about the riot that the chapter does not? Pick out two details to support the main point of the passage. What does the detail about the "Confederate battle flags" tell you about the riot?

SOUTHERN LIFE

It took a lot of courage for an African American in the 1960s to oppose an angry white crowd in the South. The United States, and the South in particular, has a long history of oppression toward African Americans. Starting in the 1600s, people from Africa were brought to North America to work as slaves. For more than 200 years, they were sold to

White students shout insults at the US Marshals on the Ole Miss campus on September 30, 1962.

Whites and African Americans ride a segregated bus in Atlanta, Georgia, in 1956. Jim Crow laws forced African Americans to sit in the back of buses.

whites. Slavery existed throughout the United States. But it was more common in the South.

Many people in the Northern states tried to get rid of slavery. But people in the South resisted. The disagreement between states led to the Civil War (1861–1865). After the war ended, slavery was outlawed. But many Southern whites did not want African Americans to be considered equal. So they created laws to control African Americans in other ways.

Jim Crow

From the 1880s to the 1960s, whites in the South created racist state laws. These became known as Jim Crow laws. Jim Crow laws segregated society. African Americans were forced to use separate facilities from whites.

In 1896 a man named Homer Plessy challenged segregation on trains. His case went to the US Supreme Court. But in *Plessy v. Ferguson*, the court ruled in favor of segregation. The decision said that if the facilities were equal in quality, segregation should be allowed.

The Origin of Jim Crow

The name "Jim Crow" came from a character played on stage. Jim Crow was played by Thomas Dartmouth "Daddy" Rice. He wore blackface, dark makeup used to make a white person look like they have dark skin. The Jim Crow character was a mean stereotype of an African-American man. The character was lazy and foolish. Other blackface characters started from Rice's character. They spread a negative image of African Americans in the United States.

Returning from Detroit

When Meredith was 15, he went on a trip to Detroit, Michigan. African Americans faced discrimination in the North. But there were not segregation laws like in the South. On the way back to Mississippi, the difference became clear. The train approached Mississippi's state line. The conductor told Meredith to move to an African-American train car. Some white passengers told Meredith to stay. But he chose to move. He was embarrassed. He cried the rest of the ride home. Meredith vowed then to fight against the poor treatment of African Americans.

Before the case, whites and African Americans were separated in places like schools, buses, and trains. After the case, new laws extended segregation to restaurants, parks, theaters, and cemeteries. Often the facilities for whites were far better than those used by African Americans. For example, state funding gave nearly 50 percent more money to white schools.

Things were not equal socially either. For example, African Americans could not call

Under Jim Crow laws, some restaurants, like this one in North Carolina, had signs over their doors saying which race could enter.

whites by their first names or accuse a white person of lying. African Americans could be lynched if they did not follow social rules. These rules and Jim Crow laws kept whites in a position of power in the South.

FURTHER EVIDENCE

Chapter Two covers Jim Crow laws and social rules in the South. It also covers the origin of Jim Crow and the use of blackface. Check out the video at the link below. It shows how blackface was used as a form of white entertainment. What does the video tell you about how African Americans were treated under Jim Crow laws?

Blackening Up
mycorelibrary.com/james-meredith

APPLYING TO OLE MISS

The University of Mississippi was not just another college in the state. Ole Miss was the pride of whites in Mississippi. And it had been segregated since it was founded in 1848. Meredith's journey to Ole Miss would be a long one. After high school graduation, it took 11 years before he would be a student there. He would spend roughly one and a half years battling to be admitted.

It was an honor for students to be accepted into Ole Miss.

Meredith and Mary June Wiggins met while he served in the US Air Force.

In the Air Force

Meredith finished high school in 1951. He lived with his aunt in Florida during his senior year. Meredith's father had sent him to a good high school there. But in 1951, there was still not much support for school integration. And Meredith could not afford to go to college. He decided to wait. He signed up for four years with the US Air Force.

While in the Air Force, Meredith took college courses to catch up in his weaker areas of study. Then, in 1954, the US Supreme Court ruled in

Brown v. Board of Education that having separate schools for African Americans and whites was unconstitutional. The decision was a step toward equality. But integration was still far off at many Southern schools.

Meredith signed up for another four-year commitment to the air force in 1955. In 1956 Meredith married Mary June Wiggins and later became a father. Starting in 1957, he was stationed in Japan for three years. There he experienced equal treatment from the Japanese. They treated him as an American soldier, not an African-American soldier.

Back in Mississippi

Meredith's tour ended in 1960. He and his wife chose to move back to Mississippi. Meredith wanted to stand up to racism in his home state. He saw education as his main tool to win that fight.

Meredith started by going to Jackson State College in Jackson, Mississippi. It was an African-American school. He already had half the

Medgar Evers, *right*, helped Meredith, *center*, secure the NAACP's assistance. Evers had applied to and been rejected by Ole Miss's law school in 1953.

credits needed for a degree. At Jackson State, Meredith met other African Americans who also wanted to fight for equal rights. He joined the National Association for the Advancement of Colored People (NAACP). Then, in 1960, John F. Kennedy became president. Kennedy wanted to help advance civil rights in the United States. It seemed to be the right time for Meredith to apply to Ole Miss.

Waiting for an Answer

On January 21, 1961, Meredith sent a letter asking for an application to Ole Miss. He then wrote a letter to Thurgood Marshall. Marshall was the director of the NAACP's Legal Defense Fund. Meredith asked for Marshall's legal help if needed in his attempt to go to Ole Miss.

Meredith filed his application on January 31. In the letter, Meredith included that he was African-American. He received a telegram

Earlier Attempts

Three men had tried to integrate Mississippi colleges in the 1950s. All three had been systematically denied. Medgar Evers applied to Ole Miss's law school in 1953. His application was rejected due to "technical errors." Clennon King applied to an Ole Miss PhD program in 1958. People at the school ordered an evaluation of King. Then they said he failed the test and sent him to a mental institution. Clyde Kennard applied to the University of Southern Mississippi in 1959. Minutes after an interview at the school, he was suspiciously arrested for speeding. He was fined and later framed for a crime. He was sentenced to seven years in prison.

four days later. It said that the school would not be considering him for admission. But it did not say his application had been denied.

The NAACP Legal Defense Fund chose to take on Meredith's case. They told him to ask to be considered for the summer session. Meredith did this. The school received his letter but did not reply. The Legal Defense Fund advised Meredith on how to completely fulfill the application's requirements. If Meredith met all of the requirements and was still denied, there would be evidence for a case against Ole Miss.

Application Denied

Meredith kept writing letters to the school asking for a response. Finally, in May, he heard back. The school had received Meredith's application. But they could not accept all of the credits from courses he had taken. They asked if Meredith still wanted to apply. He told them he did.

At the end of May, the university responded to Meredith's application. It had been denied. The school said his application had not met their requirements. His letters of recommendation were not from people who had gone to Ole Miss. All of the former Ole Miss students were white, and Meredith did not know any of them. The school also said they could not accept credits from Jackson State. The fight would have to move to court.

EXPLORE ONLINE

Chapter Three covers Meredith's application to Ole Miss. As mentioned in the chapter, Meredith wrote a letter to Thurgood Marshall. The website below shows the letter Meredith wrote. As you know, every source is different. What does the letter tell you that the chapter text does not? What information is the same? How do the two sources present information differently?

Letter from James Meredith to Thurgood Marshall

mycorelibrary.com/james-meredith

CHAPTER FOUR

GOING TO COURT

Meredith and the NAACP filed a court case against Ole Miss just a week after receiving the rejection letter. At the same time, the state began preparing its defense. It would try to prove Meredith was not rejected because of his race. The state would argue Meredith was not a serious student. They would also suggest that Meredith was a criminal.

Meredith, left, exits the courthouse with his lawyers on June 1, 1961.

Constance Baker Motley, *left*, had a successful history of working on major civil rights cases for the NAACP.

Meredith would have to prove he was denied only because of his race.

Judge Mize's Ruling

Meredith's lawyer was Constance Baker Motley of the NAACP, along with Mississippi lawyer R. Jess Brown. The judge was Sidney C. Mize, a 74-year-old who supported segregation.

On June 8, Meredith and his lawyers met with Judge Mize and three lawyers who represented the university. The purpose of the meeting was for the school's lawyers to ask Meredith questions about the complaint. Assistant Attorney General Dugas Shands asked most of the questions. Many did not have to do with the complaint. They were designed to upset and confuse Meredith. Shands asked if Meredith knew what a complaint was. He quizzed Meredith about

Meredith, center, and Motley, right, pass media crews and protesters as they approach the courthouse.

his wife, his use of credit cards, and where he got his typewriter. But it did not work. Meredith knew exactly what the lawyer was trying to do.

Meredith's first hearing took place on June 12, 1961. After the hearing, Mize refused to set a court date until he established that Meredith lived in Mississippi. The judge put off the trial for six months. He finally set a trial date for January 24, 1962. After hearing both sides, Judge Mize gave his ruling on February 3. He ruled in favor of the state. Mize found no proof Meredith was kept from attending Ole Miss because of his race.

Appealed and Overturned

Meredith's lawyers appealed the case to a higher court. They tried to get Mize's decision overruled right away so Meredith could start school in February. But Meredith had to wait for another full trial.

His case again went to court. On June 25, the court's decision was given. The majority opinion was that Meredith had been rejected by Ole Miss only because of his race. Judge Mize's decision had been overturned.

But there was another delay. A different judge ordered that a hold be placed on the decision until the US Supreme Court gave a ruling. After two weeks of waiting, President Kennedy decided to act. The Department of Justice sent a request to US Supreme Court Justice Hugo Black to set aside the hold. On September 10, Justice Black did this. He ordered that Meredith be immediately admitted to Ole Miss. On September 13, Judge Mize ordered the school not to slow Meredith's admission.

The Little Rock Nine

The US National Guard had been used before to protect African-American students attending a white school. It happened in Little Rock, Arkansas, in September 1957. Nine African-American students tried to enter an all-white school. The state's governor blocked their entrance. President Dwight D. Eisenhower ordered the National Guard and other federal troops to protect the African-American students. The students were guarded for the rest of the school year. Ernest Green became the first African-American graduate of the school in 1958.

Governor Barnett Responds

That same day, Governor Barnett responded on radio and television. He twisted the story, making the issue more about the US government overpowering state rights. He promised to do all that he could to stop integration. At the same time, President Kennedy vowed to protect Meredith's civil rights. Kennedy hoped something could be peacefully arranged. If not, the National Guard was waiting to step in.

At the time Meredith's case was filed, civil rights activists were riding buses through the South to fight segregation on public buses. They were known as Freedom Riders. A magazine article described the arrival of Freedom Riders in Jackson, Mississippi:

> *Weary Freedom Riders strode briskly through the doors into the bus station. But uniformed and plainclothes police waiting inside, snatched the passengers aside one by one and took them to a police paddy wagon parked in front of the station. . . . Gov. Ross Barnett hastily called a press conference in the state capitol building to present the state's side of the case to reporters. . . . To further show the southern viewpoint, Barnett took newsmen on a tour of the city's segregated facilities, pointing out that $57 million was spent on improving obvious Negro slum conditions.*
>
> Source: Larry A. Still. "A Bus Ride Through Mississippi." Ebony. August 1, 1961. Print. 27.

Changing Minds

Think about how the treatment of the Freedom Riders may have influenced a student's thoughts about integration at Ole Miss. Write a letter to Meredith expressing that point of view. Would the student encourage Meredith to continue fighting for equal rights? Or might the student feel threatened by Meredith's goal?

CHAPTER FIVE

INTEGRATING OLE MISS

The town of Oxford was tense in the fall of 1962. A showdown between a state and the federal government was about to begin. Governor Barnett was set to challenge President Kennedy. Many white Mississippians supported Barnett.

On September 20, ten days before the riot at Ole Miss, Meredith tried to register for the first time. That morning a 27-foot (8-m) cross was found burning on

Governor Barnett waves to cheering students as he arrives on the Ole Miss campus.

Federal marshals escort Meredith off campus after his application was rejected on September 20, 1962.

campus. This was a sign of the Ku Klux Klan, a white supremacist group. It was often used to scare African Americans. Nearly 2,000 people were gathered in front of the Lyceum by afternoon.

US Marshals escorted Meredith to the meeting. There he met Governor Barnett. The school board had made Barnett the acting registrar. It did not want to defy a federal order. Meredith asked to be admitted. Barnett denied him.

The federal government responded. It charged school officials with contempt. This meant they were disobeying a court order. Then the federal government put a restraining order on the governor, Mississippi police, and the state. This meant they could not block Meredith's enrollment at the school.

Moral Turpitude

Governor Barnett had a tool ready to deny Meredith's admission. On September 20, a local judge held a trial falsely accusing Meredith of a crime. The judge found him guilty of "moral turpitude," or going against moral standards. Meredith was not at the trial. But the state government quickly passed a law. It denied admission to any state school to a person charged with moral turpitude. The law was aimed at Meredith.

On September 25 and 26, Meredith again tried to enroll at the school. Both times US Marshals went with him. On the first day, Governor Barnett again refused

Burned cars sit smoking on the Ole Miss grounds the morning after the deadly riot.

him. On the second day, the lieutenant governor and a mob blocked Meredith's way. In response, the federal government announced it would fine Barnett $10,000 per day until he let Meredith register.

Secret Plans

While Meredith was trying to register, Governor Barnett and President Kennedy discussed the situation. The president hoped to find a way for Barnett to keep his reputation while letting Meredith attend Ole Miss. They came up with plans that might allow him to do this. And Barnett seemed to want the plans to happen. He wanted to avoid violence at the school. But in the end, Barnett did not agree to any of Kennedy's suggestions. In response, Kennedy sent in federal troops.

During the height of the riot on September 30, Kennedy addressed the country. He talked about what was happening at Ole Miss. He explained that no man and no group had the right to defy

CIVIL RIGHTS VOICES
John F. Kennedy

[I]n a government of laws . . . no man—however prominent or powerful— and no mob—however unruly or boisterous—is entitled to defy a court of law.

Born on May 29, 1917, in Massachusetts, John F. Kennedy grew up in a wealthy home. He graduated from Harvard University in 1940 with a law degree. He then served in the US Navy. In 1952 he became a US Senator. Kennedy was elected US president in 1960. During his presidency, Kennedy supported civil rights. He asked the American people to end racism in the United States. He was shot and killed on November 22, 1963.

- **January 31, 1961:** Meredith submits his application to the University of Mississippi.
- **May 25, 1961:** The University of Mississippi rejects Meredith's application.
- **September 10, 1962:** The US Supreme Court orders the University of Mississippi to admit Meredith.
- **September 20, 1962:** Meredith makes his first attempt to register at the college, but is denied.
- **September 25, 1962:** Meredith makes his second attempt to register.
- **September 26, 1962:** Meredith makes his third attempt to register.
- **September 30, 1962:** US Marshals arrive on campus to assist Meredith in registering. A riot breaks out as whites protest.
- **October 1, 1962:** The US National Guard arrives on campus. US Marshals escort Meredith to register and attend class at the University of Mississippi.

Meredith's Admission

This timeline shows the series of events that occurred during Meredith's attempts to attend the University of Mississippi. After reading about his attempts, what does this timeline tell you? Does it help you better understand the length of time it took for him to be admitted?

federal law. He said that the law would be followed in Mississippi.

After the Riot

The day after the riot, Ole Miss looked liked a battlefield. Burned cars blocked streets. The smell of tear gas stayed in the air. Federal troops were everywhere.

After Meredith's first classes on October 1, he felt satisfied. He had done what he had set out to do. But his time at Ole Miss would not be easy. He was harassed on campus. He had also become famous. He received hundreds of pieces of fan and hate mail daily. It was distracting, and it hurt his grades. But he focused, and with his credits from Jackson State, Meredith graduated on August 18, 1963.

The charges against Barnett were dropped in 1965. He never served time in jail or paid a fine for disobeying federal law.

There would be many civil rights battles ahead in the state and the South. Some would be lost. But Meredith's Ole Miss battle showed that they also could be won.

James Meredith registers to attend classes at the University of Mississippi.

Date

October 1, 1962

Key Players

James Meredith, Governor Ross Barnett, President John F. Kennedy, US Marshals, University of Mississippi

What Happened

In May 1961, the University of Mississippi denied Meredith's application. He believed it was solely because of his race. Meredith took his case to court. On September 10, 1962, the US Supreme Court ordered Ole Miss to admit Meredith. Meredith tried to register several times, but was blocked by Mississippi Governor Ross Barnett and state police. A violent riot broke out on September 30. But Meredith registered for and attended classes on October 1, 1962.

Impact

Meredith's admittance to the University of Mississippi integrated the school. Soon after, more African-American students applied and attended the college. The involvement of the US National Guard and federal marshals showed that no state government would be allowed to disobey the federal government. It also proved that the US government would be involved in civil rights issues and promote racial equality in the United States.

Why Do I Care?

James Meredith became the first African American to attend the University of Mississippi. Other schools became integrated in the South after this event as well. What do you think life in the South might be like today if Meredith had not won his battle? Do battles for equal rights still exist?

Take a Stand

This book discusses how Meredith fought to register for classes and attend the University of Mississippi. Do you think Meredith should have just finished his degree at Jackson State? Or do you think it was worth his time and effort to fight to be admitted at Ole Miss? Write a short essay explaining your opinion. Make sure to give reasons for your opinion.

Tell the Tale

Chapter Three of this book discusses Meredith's application to Ole Miss. Write 200 words that tell the story of Meredith's experience applying to the university. Be sure to set the scene, develop a sequence of events, and offer a conclusion.

You Are There

This book discusses the all-night riot on the Ole Miss campus. Imagine you are a US Marshal facing the angry protestors. How does it make you feel when they are throwing things at you and the other marshals?

GLOSSARY

Confederate flag
symbol of the Confederate States of America, which fought in favor of slavery during the Civil War

federal
a system of government in which states are united under a central body, while still having state powers and governments

integrate
to make open to all cultures and races

lynch
to kill someone without a legal trial

oppression
prolonged cruel or unfair treatment

racism
a belief that race defines certain values and traits of people, and that one race is more important than another

registrar
a person at a school who signs people up for classes

reputation
how others perceive a person's worth and character

segregation
the practice of keeping different races apart from each other

white supremacy
a belief that white people are better than other races of people

LEARN MORE

Books

Adler, David. *Heroes for Civil Rights.* New York: Holiday House, 2008.

Bausum, Ann. *Freedom Riders: John Lewis and Jim Zwerg on the Front Lines of the Civil Rights Movement.* Washington, DC: National Geographic, 2006.

Smith, Charles R. *28 Days: Moments in Black History that Changed the World.* New York: Roaring Brook Press, 2015.

Websites

To learn more about Stories of the Civil Rights Movement, visit **booklinks.abdopublishing.com**. These links are routinely monitored and updated to provide the most current information available.

Visit **mycorelibrary.com** for free additional tools for teachers and students.

INDEX

ABOUT THE AUTHOR

Karen Latchana Kenney is the author of more than 100 books for children. She loves writing about civil rights. It inspires her to stand up for what is right even if it is not the accepted thing to do. Kenney lives in Minneapolis, Minnesota.